FOR LOVE AND FOR DEATH

(A BOOK OF POEMS)

YASH NAGLE

Dedicated to the people who, in their own ways, have made my life better. Thank you for your love, for your indifference, for your hate, and for the lessons you taught me. I will forever carry your imprints in the deepest recesses of my being.

Contents

I

"4 AM, Unrequited love, Despair"

Perhaps this emptiness is my home,
All I am left with is your hue,
your ghost.
The silence speaks of you,
For your love it yearns,
If only you could hear its words.
Perhaps, I could tell you what it says,
Perhaps, someday,
Perhaps, this emptiness is my home,
For it's all I have ever known.

II

"Bad coffee, Vast Ocean, Loneliness"

The sea teaches silence,
The thundering
Shimmering waves pull
Me deep within myself.
Time loses meaning,
Only thought remains-
One with the never
Ending vastness,
And in the reflections
Iridescent I find myself
Broken and restless,
Awaiting a revelation that
Ultimately escapes me.

III

"Writer's block, Insomnia, Jazz"

Dear Abby,
The world burns and the fire spreads,
There's no more room in my head,
Same old routine, day and night,
Dreams of a shadow, a glimmer of light.
Dear Abby,
Do you remember when the stars had stories to tell?
Do you remember our regrets?
Do you remember?
The lies we weaved and our false beliefs,
Do you remember our song that painted the night?

IV

"Heartbroken"

I am sitting alone in a coffee shop.
In front of me are lovers,
Lost souls who found heaven in a
Quaint quiet corner of an otherwise chaotic city.
Time to them is but a fickle concept,
An enemy moral who has shown mercy.
They search for smiles in each other's eyes,
Beauty they never found before.
They search for stories in each other's voices,
Pain and hurt and heartbreak,
The color of their being.
The sun sets and they see the world again,
Alone, like me, like they were before,
The crowds gather on the streets,
And they look for each other,
Nowhere to be found.

V

"A degenerate, A victim, A tragedy"

There lay an old brick house within the sea,
The rain drummed a familiar melody.
The voices from the old brick house
Travel across the sea,
They make the weeds and the fish
Dream of a rather strange memory-
Smoke and ash and anger,
Blood, bottles, and pain.
A scream suppressed and disguised as a prayer.
Regrets.
A poem written abruptly to justify the end.

VI

"Bob Dylan makes me think of her"

My song travels on the ripples of water green,
My love, it carries for her to see,
To the coast of a land blind to me,
And when she looks at the sea,
She will find my song sailing in the wind,
And when she smiles and sends me a kiss,
The winds will come back to me,
With whispers of her song,
The song her heart sings when she thinks of me.

VII

"Miserable, Heavy-hearted, Down in the dumps"

Happiness now costs more,
My words and my soul,
I look for it beneath the bushes,
I look in little pockets of the sun,
I look for it in poems I abandoned,
But the price I pay never seems to change,
And I am running out of words to say,
I am running out of worlds to create,
And I don't have much of a soul to spend.

VIII

"Memento Mori"

What happens after I die?
Will I be the sky?
Or will I be a drop of rain that pierces the castles high?
Will I be the wind flying across the sea?
Or will I be a blade of grass dancing on my whim?
Will I be one of autumn's last leaves?
Maybe I will be a song of spring,
Maybe I will be a happy dream,
Or maybe I will be the sun rising above the Serengeti.

IX

"I don't think she understands love"

Love is but a thousand heartbreaks,
It is melancholy and joy,
It is hope and sorrow,
It is ecstasy.
Love is a song sung
By a drunk man waiting
For a rapture to sweep him off his feet.

X

"I don't think I understand love"

A broken heart can never be mended
Because love etches itself in your existence.
Go astray and drift if you must
To worlds previously familiar,
The scars of love will always be inked on your palms,
They shall remind you that love,
However sweet its strain, is a cruel bard,
If you must, ask the stars,
They could tell you the tales of those who sang of love
And died of a broken heart.

The End